The New City Catechism

The New City Catechism

52 Questions
& Answers
for Our Hearts
& Minds

Introduction by
Kathy Keller

 CROSSWAY®

WHEATON, ILLINOIS

The New City Catechism:
52 Questions and Answers for Our
Hearts and Minds

Copyright © 2017 by The Gospel
Coalition and Redeemer Presbyterian
Church

Published by
Crossway
1300 Crescent Street
Wheaton, Illinois 60187

This publication was made possible
through the support of a grant from
the John Templeton Foundation.
The opinions expressed in this
publication are those of the publisher
and do not necessarily reflect
the views of the John Templeton
Foundation.

Design:
Matthew Wahl

First printing 2017
Printed in China

Trade paperback ISBN:
978-1-4335-5507-7
ePub ISBN: 978-1-4335-5510-7
PDF ISBN: 978-1-4335-5508-4
Mobipocket ISBN: 978-1-4335-5509-1

Crossway is a publishing ministry of
Good News Publishers.

RRDS 29 28 27 26 25 24 23 22 21 20 19
18 17 16 15 14 13 12 11 10 9 8 7 6 5 4

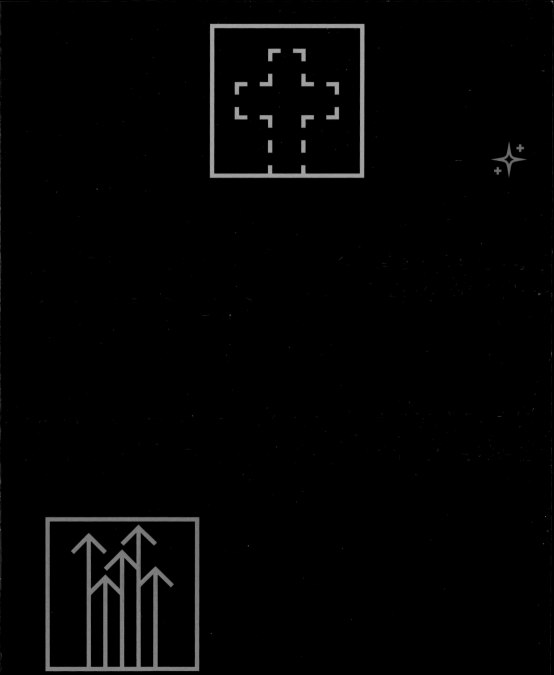

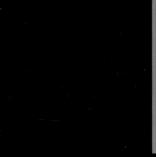

Introduction
by Kathy Keller

"Catechism — with *our* kids?" Years ago that was my response when someone suggested that we begin doing a catechism with our very young, very active boys. But, to my amazement, it was a truly wonderful experience.

We used the *Catechism for Young Children*, a highly simplified version based on the *Westminster Shorter Catechism*. The first questions are very easy, and the answers so short that even an eighteen-month-old can answer triumphantly "God!" when asked "Who made you?" and "Everything" to the second question, "What else did God make?" We discovered that our kids loved the question/answer dynamic; to them it was almost a game, through which they could experience a legitimate sense of achievement.

My first encounter with teaching a catechism to children was even more counterintuitive. As a seminary student I spent one summer working for a church in a gang-infested part of Philadelphia. There I heard of a young pastor in an even more troubled area of the city who had developed a very successful ministry to children. It met on Saturdays and attracted hundreds of elementary and middle school kids. I decided to go see the program in action.

I'm not sure what I expected — warm-hearted volunteers dispensing Kool-Aid, hugs, and Jesus stories? What I found, to my slack-jawed amazement, was a building with more than two hundred kids in it, divided by age group, learning the catechism! I must admit that very few things have surprised me more. I had never given a thought to the catechism as a modern-day teaching tool, and even if I had, it would not have occurred to me to use it in these circumstances.

The pastor was used to the shocked disbelief and surprised questions: "Why on earth are you having them memorize a catechism? Don't they need the basic gospel message? When do you get to that"? I have still not forgotten his answer:

> These kids know nothing whatsoever about God, or Jesus, or sin. They've never even heard the words, except as curse words. We're building a framework in their minds of words and ideas and concepts, so that when we do tell them about sin and the Savior who came to die for it, there is a way for them to understand what we are saying.

I went away chastened, but not entirely convinced. Maybe so, but it still seemed so, so *medieval* to have children memorizing the catechism, no matter how deprived their spiritual education had been. A few weeks later I changed my mind.

I had developed a mentor relationship with a twelve-year-old girl from the neighborhood, and I was sharing the gospel with her, or so I thought. Waxing eloquent, I said, "Do you know what Easter means?" She thought seriously for a moment, and then answered, "It was either when that guy was born or when he died, I forget." I realized she had no framework to understand my words. I wish I'd started her on a catechism instead.

7

One last personal story from my family. Jonathan, our youngest, was waiting for me to pick him up at his babysitter's house. As he stared pensively out the window, she asked him, "What are you thinking about?" Unbeknownst to her, this triggered the adult-asks-a-question-and-I-provide-an-answer part of his brain, so his answer was (taken from the pages of the catechism) "God." "What are you thinking about God?" she responded in surprise, and got the even more surprising answer (comprising the second and third catechism answers): "How he made all things for his own glory." She almost fell over – she thought she was in the presence of a prodigy. Really, it was just the catechism.

Time and Commitment

Stories aside, how do people in the real world, with real twenty-first-century families, find the time or commitment to do something like a catechism? It's a challenge. Most families, on their own, stop and restart several times. (We did, too.) It is so much easier if there is a church-sponsored program, or small group accountability, where each week the next question and answer will be memorized for recitation. One mother at our church wrote:

> We have several ways that catechism has fit into our family lives . . . some more successful than others, but we do feel it is very important. We've used a catechism for bed-time devotionals with our children. We have started and stopped memorizing catechisms as a family several times. And I taught it as a

class at church for 4th/5th-graders. The positive effect catechesis has had on our family is: summarizing God's truths into digestible questions and answers so that as our children experience life and the world around them, they are able to understand how God has worked through time and history, how he will work in their lives and in the future of this world and mankind. As we walk through the difficult questions in life, the catechism is often the guide to which we are able to direct our children to the truths in Scripture.

The key is becoming convinced that you are furnishing your child with the mental foundation on which the rest of his or her spiritual life will be built. Or, to switch metaphors, you are laying the kindling and the logs in the fireplace, so that when the spark of the Holy Spirit ignites your child's heart, there will be a steady, mature blaze.

Memorization Tips

- Read the question and answer out loud, and repeat, repeat, repeat.
- Read the question and answer out loud, then try to repeat them without looking. Repeat.
- Read aloud all part 1 questions and answers (then part 2, then part 3) while physically moving about. The combination of movement and speech strengthens a person's ability to recall text.
- Record yourself saying all part 1 questions and answers (then part 2, then part 3) and listen to them during everyday activities such as workouts, chores, and so on.
- Write the questions and answers on cards and tape them in a conspicuous area. Read them aloud every time you see them.
- Make flash cards with the question on one side and the answer on the other, and test yourself. Children can color these in and draw pictures on them.
- Review the question and answer at night and in the morning. For children spend a few minutes at bedtime helping them remember the answer, then repeat at breakfast the next morning.
- Write out the question and answer. Repeat. The process of writing helps a person's ability to recall text.
- Drill the questions and answers with another person as often as possible.
- Visit **www.newcitycatechism.com** to find songs and other resources to help with learning *The New City Catechism*.

Our Response to God

Children are constantly learning. Their inquiring minds soak up information at a spectacular rate. They are trying to make sense of a complex and ever-changing world, seeking to acquire the skills to survive – and even thrive – in life. As they learn, a framework of understanding is established in their minds. This is called a worldview. All children and adults observe and interact with the world through their personal worldview. It is a thrilling and great responsibility to raise children and shape their understanding of the world, how it works, and their unique purpose in it. To catechize children is to build their worldview, to teach them from Scripture about the world, and to inform their interactions with those they will live, play, learn, and work alongside.

You will notice that each catechism question has a symbol that corresponds to one of the Christian virtues listed on page 11. Each question and corresponding answer is derived directly from Scripture; as children are catechized, they are learning to bury the truths of Scripture deep in their hearts. The virtue symbols are simply guides to help families talk about how to respond to the Word of God, and they correspond to The New City Catechism Curriculum (Crossway 2018). The emphasis and intention of *The New City Catechism* is to shape and affect the hearts of the children who learn it, with the hope that the catechism will contribute greatly to the nurture of godly, mature, and virtuous young men and women.

It is our hope that as families work together to learn the fifty-two questions and answers found in this book, they will increase not only in knowledge, but in the fruit of the Spirit, as they grow to love God with all of their hearts.

And these words that I command you today shall be on your heart. You shall teach them diligently to your children, and shall talk of them when you sit in your house, and when you walk by the way, and when you lie down, and when you rise. You shall bind them as a sign on your hand, and they shall be as frontlets between your eyes. You shall write them on the doorposts of your house and on your gates. (Deut. 6:6–9)

— Melanie Lacy
   Director of Theology for Children
   and Youth, Oak Hill College

Virtues Key

Awe

As children gain an increasing awareness of God, they will correctly understand themselves as ones who have been created for relationship with God and others.

Forgiveness

As children clearly comprehend the amazing forgiveness that has been provided for them through Christ's sacrificial death on the cross, they will develop an active forgiving nature.

Gratitude

As children realize the goodness and grace of God in their own lives, a disposition of gratitude is developed; this nurtures a grateful spirit and causes children to act in generous ways toward others.

Honesty

As children recognize the truth of the gospel and the holiness of God, they will desire to live in a transparent and honest way that will greatly benefit their relationship with God and others.

Hope

As children come to understand God's eternal plans and provision, they will begin to know the hope that God is presently at work in them making them more like Jesus, and that one day they will be with him forever.

Humility

As children observe the humility displayed in Jesus's life, they will be shaped to be increasingly inclined to put the needs of others before their own. They should be willing to sacrifice personal gain and status for the sake of others.

Joy

As children come to know and understand the perfection, power, and provision of God, they will develop a joyful disposition. This will allow them to find contentment in God and his promises rather than fleeting happiness that comes from external factors and experiences.

Love

As children comprehend the unconditional, redemptive love of God, their ability to love and propensity for love will increase and influence their own familial and peer relationships.

Perseverance

As children understand the work of the Spirit in their lives and the hope of eternal glory, a spirit of perseverance grows; they will be established to face the trials and difficulties of life confident in the power and provision of God.

Trust

As children learn great truths about the triune God and the Scriptures, a robust and trustworthy worldview is established through which the world may be encountered.

The large catechism question is easy to read quickly.

Question 24

Why was it necessary for Christ, the Redeemer, to die?

The illustrations throughout the book are visual depictions of the questions and answers in the catechism. Each illustration was designed to help visual learners with memorization.

Answer

Since death is the punishment for sin, Christ
died willingly in our place
to deliver us from the
power and penalty of sin
and bring us back to God.
By his substitutionary
atoning death, he alone
redeems us from hell
and gains for us forgive-
ness of sin, righteousness,
and everlasting life.

The highlighted portion is
a more concise answer
designed to be memorized
by younger children.

The icon represents a
response to God that flows
from each question.
A key to the icons can be
found on page 11.

Colossians 1:21–22
And you, who once were alienated
and hostile in mind, doing evil deeds, he
has now reconciled in his body of flesh
by his death, in order to present you holy
and blameless and above reproach
before him.

Supporting Scripture
passage.

Part 1

God,
Creation & Fall,
Law

What is our only hope in life and death?

Answer

That we are not our own
but belong, body and soul,
both in life and death,
to God and to our Savior
Jesus Christ.

Romans 14:7–8
For none of us lives to himself, and none
of us dies to himself. For if we live, we live
to the Lord, and if we die, we die to the
Lord. So then, whether we live or whether
we die, we are the Lord's.

What is God?

Answer

God is the creator and sustainer of everyone and everything. He is eternal, infinite, and unchangeable in his power and perfection, goodness and glory, wisdom, justice, and truth. Nothing happens except through him and by his will.

Psalm 86:8–10, 15
There is none like you among the gods, O Lord, nor are there any works like yours. All the nations you have made shall come and worship before you, O Lord, and shall glorify your name. For you are great and do wondrous things; you alone are God…. But you, O Lord, are a God merciful and gracious, slow to anger and abounding in steadfast love and faithfulness.

How many persons are there in God?

Answer

There are three persons in the one true and living God: the Father, the Son, and the Holy Spirit. They are the same in substance, equal in power and glory.

2 Corinthians 13:14
The grace of the Lord Jesus Christ and the love of God and the fellowship of the Holy Spirit be with you all.

How and why did God create us?

Answer

God created us male and female in his own image to know him, love him, live with him, and glorify him. And it is right that we who were created by God should live to his glory.

Genesis 1:27
So God created man in his own image, in the image of God he created him; male and female he created them.

What else did God create?

Answer

God created all things by his powerful Word, and all his creation was very good; everything flourished under his loving rule.

Genesis 1:31
And God saw everything that he had made, and behold, it was very good.

Question 6

How can we glorify God?

Answer

We glorify God by enjoying him, loving him, trusting him, and by obeying his will, commands, and law.

Deuteronomy 11:1
You shall therefore love the LORD your God and keep his charge, his statutes, his rules, and his commandments always.

What does the law of God require?

Answer

Personal, perfect, and perpetual obedience; that we love God with all our heart, soul, mind, and strength; and love our neighbor as ourselves. What God forbids should never be done and what God commands should always be done.

Matthew 22:37–40
And [Jesus] said to him, "You shall love the Lord your God with all your heart and with all your soul and with all your mind. This is the great and first commandment. And a second is like it: You shall love your neighbor as yourself. On these two commandments depend all the Law and the Prophets."

What is the law of God stated in the Ten Commandments?

Answer

You shall have no other gods before me. You shall not make for yourself an idol in the form of anything in heaven above or on the earth beneath or in the waters below — you shall not bow down to them or worship them. You shall not misuse the name of the LORD your God. Remember the Sabbath day by keeping it holy. Honor your father and your mother. You shall not murder. You shall not commit adultery. You shall not steal. You shall not give false testimony. You shall not covet.

Exodus 20:3
You shall have no other gods before me.

What does God require in the first, second, and third commandments?

Answer

First, that we know and trust God as the only true and living God. Second, that we avoid all idolatry and do not worship God improperly. Third, that we treat God's name with fear and reverence, honoring also his Word and works.

Deuteronomy 6:13–14
It is the LORD your God you shall fear. Him you shall serve and by his name you shall swear. You shall not go after other gods, the gods of the peoples who are around you.

What does God require in the fourth and fifth commandments?

Answer

Fourth, that on the Sabbath day we spend time in public and private worship of God, rest from routine employment, serve the Lord and others, and so anticipate the eternal Sabbath. Fifth, that we love and honor our father and our mother, submitting to their godly discipline and direction.

Leviticus 19:3
Every one of you shall revere his mother and his father, and you shall keep my Sabbaths: I am the LORD your God.

What does God require in the sixth, seventh, and eighth commandments?

Answer

Sixth, that we do not hurt, or hate, or be hostile to our neighbor, but be patient and peaceful, pursuing even our enemies with love. Seventh, that we abstain from sexual immorality and live purely and faithfully, whether in marriage or in single life, avoiding all impure actions, looks, words, thoughts, or desires, and whatever might lead to them. Eighth, that we do not take without permission that which belongs to someone else, nor withhold any good from someone we might benefit.

Romans 13:9
For the commandments, "You shall not commit adultery, You shall not murder, You shall not steal, You shall not covet," and any other commandment, are summed up in this word: "You shall love your neighbor as yourself."

What does God require in the ninth and tenth commandments?

Answer

Ninth, that we do not lie or deceive, but speak the truth in love. Tenth, that we are content, not envying anyone or resenting what God has given them or us.

James 2:8
If you really fulfill the royal law according to the Scripture, "You shall love your neighbor as yourself," you are doing well.

Can anyone keep the law of God perfectly?

Answer

Since the fall, no mere human has been able to keep the law of God perfectly, but consistently breaks it in thought, word, and deed.

Romans 3:10–12
None is righteous, no, not one; no one understands; no one seeks for God. All have turned aside; together they have become worthless; no one does good, not even one.

Did God create us unable to keep his law?

Answer

No, but because of the disobedience of our first parents, Adam and Eve, all of creation is fallen; we are all born in sin and guilt, corrupt in our nature and unable to keep God's law.

Romans 5:12
Therefore, just as sin came into the world through one man, and death through sin, and so death spread to all men because all sinned.

Since no one can keep the law, what is its purpose?

Answer

That we may know the holy nature and will of God, and the sinful nature and disobedience of our hearts; and thus our need of a Savior. The law also teaches and exhorts us to live a life worthy of our Savior.

Romans 3:20
For by works of the law no human being will be justified in his sight, since through the law comes knowledge of sin.

What is sin?

Answer

Sin is rejecting or ignoring God in the world he created, rebelling against him by living without reference to him, not being or doing what he requires in his law – resulting in our death and the disintegration of all creation.

1 John 3:4
Everyone who makes a practice of sinning also practices lawlessness; sin is lawlessness.

What is idolatry?

Answer

Idolatry is trusting in created things rather than the Creator for our hope and happiness, significance and security.

Romans 1:21, 25
For although they knew God, they did not honor him as God or give thanks to him, but they became futile in their thinking, and their foolish hearts were darkened.... They exchanged the truth about God for a lie and worshiped and served the creature rather than the Creator.

Will God allow our disobedience and idolatry to go unpunished?

Answer

No, every sin is against the sovereignty, holiness, and goodness of God, and against his righteous law, and God is righteously angry with our sins and will punish them in his just judgment both in this life, and in the life to come.

Ephesians 5:5–6
For you may be sure of this, that everyone who is sexually immoral or impure, or who is covetous (that is, an idolater), has no inheritance in the kingdom of Christ and God. Let no one deceive you with empty words, for because of these things the wrath of God comes upon the sons of disobedience.

Is there any way to escape punishment and be brought back into God's favor?

Answer

Yes, to satisfy his justice, God himself, out of mere mercy, reconciles us to himself and delivers us from sin and from the punishment for sin, by a Redeemer.

Isaiah 53:10–11
Yet it was the will of the LORD to crush him; he has put him to grief; when his soul makes an offering for guilt, he shall see his offspring; he shall prolong his days; the will of the LORD shall prosper in his hand. Out of the anguish of his soul he shall see and be satisfied; by his knowledge shall the righteous one, my servant, make many to be accounted righteous, and he shall bear their iniquities.

Who is the Redeemer?

Answer

The only Redeemer is the Lord Jesus Christ, the eternal Son of God, in whom God became man and bore the penalty for sin himself.

1 Timothy 2:5
For there is one God, and there is one mediator between God and men, the man Christ Jesus.

Part 2

Christ, Redemption, Grace

What sort of Redeemer is needed to bring us back to God?

Answer

One who is truly human and also truly God.

Isaiah 9:6
For to us a child is born, to us a son is given; and the government shall be upon his shoulder, and his name shall be called Wonderful Counselor, Mighty God, Everlasting Father, Prince of Peace.

Why must the Redeemer be truly human?

Answer

That in human nature he might on our behalf perfectly obey the whole law and suffer the punishment for human sin; and also that he might sympathize with our weaknesses.

Hebrews 2:17
Therefore he had to be made like his brothers in every respect, so that he might become a merciful and faithful high priest in the service of God, to make propitiation for the sins of the people.

Why must the Redeemer be truly God?

Answer

That because of his divine nature his obedience and suffering would be perfect and effective; and also that he would be able to bear the righteous anger of God against sin and yet overcome death.

Acts 2:24
God raised him up, loosing the pangs of death, because it was not possible for him to be held by it.

Why was it necessary for Christ, the Redeemer, to die?

Answer

Since death is the punishment for sin, Christ died willingly in our place to deliver us from the power and penalty of sin and bring us back to God. By his substitutionary atoning death, he alone redeems us from hell and gains for us forgiveness of sin, righteousness, and everlasting life.

Colossians 1:21–22
And you, who once were alienated and hostile in mind, doing evil deeds, he has now reconciled in his body of flesh by his death, in order to present you holy and blameless and above reproach before him.

Does Christ's death mean all our sins can be forgiven?

Answer

Yes, because Christ's death on the cross fully paid the penalty for our sin, God graciously imputes Christ's righteousness to us as if it were our own and will remember our sins no more.

2 Corinthians 5:21
For our sake he made him to be sin who knew no sin, so that in him we might become the righteousness of God.

Question 26

What else does Christ's death redeem?

Answer

Christ's death is the beginning of the redemption and renewal of every part of fallen creation, as he powerfully directs all things for his own glory and creation's good.

Colossians 1:19–20
For in him all the fullness of God was pleased to dwell, and through him to reconcile to himself all things, whether on earth or in heaven, making peace by the blood of his cross.

Are all people, just as they were lost through Adam, saved through Christ?

Answer

No, only those who are elected by God and united to Christ by faith. Nevertheless God in his mercy demonstrates common grace even to those who are not elect, by restraining the effects of sin and enabling works of culture for human well-being.

Romans 5:17
For if, because of one man's trespass, death reigned through that one man, much more will those who receive the abundance of grace and the free gift of righteousness reign in life through the one man Jesus Christ.

What happens after death to those not united to Christ by faith?

Answer

At the day of judgment they will receive the fearful but just sentence of condemnation pronounced against them. They will be cast out from the favorable presence of God, into hell, to be justly and grievously punished, forever.

John 3:16–18, 36

For God so loved the world, that he gave his only Son, that whoever believes in him should not perish but have eternal life. For God did not send his Son into the world to condemn the world, but in order that the world might be saved through him. Whoever believes in him is not condemned, but whoever does not believe is condemned already, because he has not believed in the name of the only Son of God. . . . Whoever believes in the Son has eternal life; whoever does not obey the Son shall not see life, but the wrath of God remains on him.

How can we be saved?

Answer

Only by faith in Jesus Christ and in his substitutionary atoning death on the cross; so even though we are guilty of having disobeyed God and are still inclined to all evil, nevertheless, God, without any merit of our own but only by pure grace, imputes to us the perfect righteousness of Christ when we repent and believe in him.

Ephesians 2:8–9
For by grace you have been saved through faith. And this is not your own doing; it is the gift of God, not a result of works, so that no one may boast.

What is faith in Jesus Christ?

Answer

Faith in Jesus Christ is acknowledging the truth of everything that God has revealed in his Word, trusting in him, and also receiving and resting on him alone for salvation as he is offered to us in the gospel.

Galatians 2:20
I have been crucified with Christ. It is no longer I who live, but Christ who lives in me. And the life I now live in the flesh I live by faith in the Son of God, who loved me and gave himself for me.

What do we believe by true faith?

Answer

Everything taught to us in the gospel. The Apostles' Creed expresses what we believe in these words: We believe in God the Father Almighty, Maker of heaven and earth; and in Jesus Christ his only Son our Lord, who was conceived by the Holy Spirit, born of the virgin Mary, suffered under Pontius Pilate, was crucified, died, and was buried. He descended into hell. The third day he rose again from the dead. He ascended into heaven, and is seated at the right hand of God the Father Almighty; from there he will come to judge the living and the dead. We believe in the Holy Spirit, the holy catholic church, the communion of saints, the forgiveness of sins, the resurrection of the body, and the life everlasting.

Jude 3
I found it necessary to write appealing to you to contend for the faith that was once for all delivered to the saints.

What do justification and sanctification mean?

Answer

Justification means our declared righteousness before God, made possible by Christ's death and resurrection for us. Sanctification means our gradual, growing righteousness, made possible by the Spirit's work in us.

1 Peter 1:1–2

To those who are elect exiles…according to the foreknowledge of God the Father, in the sanctification of the Spirit, for obedience to Jesus Christ and for sprinkling with his blood: May grace and peace be multiplied to you.

Should those who have faith in Christ seek their salvation through their own works, or anywhere else?

Answer

No, they should not,
as everything necessary
to salvation is found in
Christ. To seek salvation
through good works
is a denial that Christ is
the only Redeemer
and Savior.

Galatians 2:16
Yet we know that a person is not justified
by works of the law but through faith
in Jesus Christ, so we also have believed
in Christ Jesus, in order to be justified
by faith in Christ and not by works of the
law, because by works of the law no
one will be justified.

Since we are redeemed by grace alone, through Christ alone, must we still do good works and obey God's Word?

Answer

Yes, because Christ, having redeemed us by his blood, also renews us by his Spirit; so that our lives may show love and gratitude to God; so that we may be assured of our faith by the fruits; and so that by our godly behavior others may be won to Christ.

1 Peter 2:9–12
But you are a chosen race, a royal priesthood, a holy nation, a people for his own possession, that you may proclaim the excellencies of him who called you out of darkness into his marvelous light. Once you were not a people, but now you are God's people; once you had not received mercy, but now you have received mercy. Beloved, I urge you as sojourners and exiles to abstain from the passions of the flesh, which wage war against your soul. Keep your conduct among the Gentiles honorable, so that when they speak against you as evildoers, they may see your good deeds and glorify God on the day of visitation.

Since we are redeemed by grace alone, through faith alone, where does this faith come from?

Answer

All the gifts we receive from Christ we receive through the Holy Spirit, including faith itself.

Titus 3:4–6
But when the goodness and loving kindness of God our Savior appeared, he saved us, not because of works done by us in righteousness, but according to his own mercy, by the washing of regeneration and renewal of the Holy Spirit, whom he poured out on us richly through Jesus Christ our Savior.

Part 3

Spirit, Restoration, Growing in Grace

What do we believe about the Holy Spirit?

Answer

That he is God, coeternal with the Father and the Son, and that God grants him irrevocably to all who believe.

John 14:16–17
And I will ask the Father, and he will give you another Helper, to be with you forever, even the Spirit of truth, whom the world cannot receive, because it neither sees him nor knows him. You know him, for he dwells with you and will be in you.

How does the Holy Spirit help us?

Answer

The Holy Spirit convicts us of our sin, comforts us, guides us, gives us spiritual gifts and the desire to obey God; and he enables us to pray and to understand God's Word.

Ephesians 6:17–18
And take the helmet of salvation, and the sword of the Spirit, which is the word of God, praying at all times in the Spirit, with all prayer and supplication. To that end keep alert with all perseverance, making supplication for all the saints.

What is prayer?

Answer

Prayer is pouring out our hearts to God in praise, petition, confession of sin, and thanksgiving.

Psalm 62:8
Trust in him at all times, O people; pour out your heart before him; God is a refuge for us.

With what attitude should we pray?

Answer

With love, perseverance, and gratefulness; in humble submission to God's will, knowing that, for the sake of Christ, he always hears our prayers.

Philippians 4:6
Do not be anxious about anything, but in everything by prayer and supplication with thanksgiving let your requests be made known to God.

What should we pray?

Answer

The whole Word of God directs and inspires us in what we should pray, including the prayer Jesus himself taught us.

Ephesians 3:14–21
For this reason I bow my knees before the Father, from whom every family in heaven and on earth is named, that according to the riches of his glory he may grant you to be strengthened with power through his Spirit in your inner being, so that Christ may dwell in your hearts through faith – that you, being rooted and grounded in love, may have strength to comprehend with all the saints what is the breadth and length and height and depth, and to know the love of Christ that surpasses knowledge, that you may be filled with all the fullness of God. Now to him who is able to do far more abundantly than all that we ask or think, according to the power at work within us, to him be glory in the church and in Christ Jesus throughout all generations, forever and ever. Amen.

What is the Lord's Prayer?

Answer

Our Father in heaven, hallowed be your name, your kingdom come, your will be done, on earth as it is in heaven. Give us today our daily bread. And forgive us our debts, as we also have forgiven our debtors. And lead us not into temptation, but deliver us from evil.

Matthew 6:9
Pray then like this: "Our Father in heaven, hallowed be your name...."

How is the Word of God to be read and heard?

Answer

With diligence, preparation, and prayer; so that we may accept it with faith, store it in our hearts, and practice it in our lives.

2 Timothy 3:16–17
All Scripture is breathed out by God and profitable for teaching, for reproof, for correction, and for training in righteousness, that the man of God may be complete, equipped for every good work.

What are the sacraments or ordinances?

Answer

The sacraments or ordinances given by God and instituted by Christ, namely baptism and the Lord's Supper, are visible signs and seals that we are bound together as a community of faith by his death and resurrection. By our use of them the Holy Spirit more fully declares and seals the promises of the gospel to us.

Romans 6:4
We were buried therefore with him by baptism into death, in order that, just as Christ was raised from the dead by the glory of the Father, we too might walk in newness of life.

What is baptism?

Answer

Baptism is the washing with water in the name of the Father, the Son, and the Holy Spirit; it signifies and seals our adoption into Christ, our cleansing from sin, and our commitment to belong to the Lord and to his church.

Matthew 28:19
Go therefore and make disciples of all nations, baptizing them in the name of the Father and of the Son and of the Holy Spirit....

Is baptism with water the washing away of sin itself?

Answer

No, only the blood of Christ and the renewal of the Holy Spirit can cleanse us from sin.

Luke 3:16
John answered them all, saying, "I baptize you with water, but he who is mightier than I is coming, the strap of whose sandals I am not worthy to untie. He will baptize you with the Holy Spirit and fire."

What is the Lord's Supper?

Answer

Christk commanded all Christians to eat bread and to drink from the cup in thankful remembrance of him and his death. The Lord's Supper is a celebration of the presence of God in our midst; bringing us into communion with God and with one another; feeding and nourishing our souls. It also anticipates the day when we will eat and drink with Christ in his Father's kingdom.

1 Corinthians 11:23–26
For I received from the Lord what I also delivered to you, that the Lord Jesus on the night when he was betrayed took bread, and when he had given thanks, he broke it, and said, "This is my body which is for you. Do this in remembrance of me." In the same way also he took the cup, after supper, saying, "This cup is the new covenant in my blood. Do this, as often as you drink it, in remembrance of me." For as often as you eat this bread and drink the cup, you proclaim the Lord's death until he comes.

Does the Lord's Supper add anything to Christ's atoning work?

Answer

No, Christ died once for all. The Lord's Supper is a covenant meal celebrating Christ's atoning work; as it is also a means of strengthening our faith as we look to him, and a foretaste of the future feast. But those who take part with unrepentant hearts eat and drink judgment on themselves.

1 Peter 3:18
For Christ also suffered once for sins, the righteous for the unrighteous, that he might bring us to God.

What is the church?

Answer

God chooses and preserves for himself a community elected for eternal life and united by faith, who love, follow, learn from, and worship God together. God sends out this community to proclaim the gospel and prefigure Christ's kingdom by the quality of their life together and their love for one another.

2 Thessalonians 2:13
But we ought always to give thanks to God for you, brothers beloved by the Lord, because God chose you as the firstfruits to be saved, through sanctification by the Spirit and belief in the truth.

Where is Christ now?

Answer

Christ rose bodily from the grave on the third day after his death and is seated at the right hand of the Father, ruling his kingdom and interceding for us, until he returns to judge and renew the whole world.

Ephesians 1:20–21
He raised him from the dead and seated him at his right hand in the heavenly places, far above all rule and authority and power and dominion, and above every name that is named, not only in this age but also in the one to come.

Question 50

What does Christ's resurrection mean for us?

Answer

Christ triumphed over sin and death by being physically resurrected, so that all who trust in him are raised to new life in this world and to everlasting life in the world to come. Just as we will one day be resurrected, so this world will one day be restored. But those who do not trust in Christ will be raised to everlasting death.

1 Thessalonians 4:13–14
But we do not want you to be uninformed, brothers, about those who are asleep, that you may not grieve as others do who have no hope. For since we believe that Jesus died and rose again, even so, through Jesus, God will bring with him those who have fallen asleep.

Of what advantage to us is Christ's ascension?

Answer

Christ physically ascended on our behalf, just as he came down to earth physically on our account, and he is now advocating for us in the presence of his Father, preparing a place for us, and also sends us his Spirit.

Romans 8:34

Who is to condemn? Christ Jesus is the one who died — more than that, who was raised — who is at the right hand of God, who indeed is interceding for us.

Question 52

What hope does everlasting life hold for us?

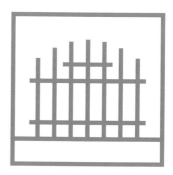

Answer

It reminds us that this present fallen world is not all there is; soon we will live with and enjoy God forever in the new city, in the new heaven and the new earth, where we will be fully and forever freed from all sin and will inhabit renewed, resurrection bodies in a renewed, restored creation.

Revelation 21:1–4

Then I saw a new heaven and a new earth, for the first heaven and the first earth had passed away, and the sea was no more. And I saw the holy city, new Jerusalem, coming down out of heaven from God, prepared as a bride adorned for her husband. And I heard a loud voice from the throne saying, "Behold, the dwelling place of God is with man. He will dwell with them, and they will be his people, and God himself will be with them as their God. He will wipe away every tear from their eyes, and death shall be no more, neither shall there be mourning, nor crying, nor pain anymore, for the former things have passed away."

Review

Writing is a helpful tool to aid memorization. Use this section for review by writing out the answers to each question and then checking them against the book.

1. What is our only hope in life and death?

 2. What is God?

 3. How many persons are there in God?

 4. How and why did God create us?

 5. What else did God create?

 6. How can we glorify God?

 7. What does the law of God require?

 8. What is the law of God stated in the Ten Commandments?

 9. What does God require in the first, second, and third commandments?

 10. What does God require in the fourth and fifth commandments?

 11. What does God require in the sixth, seventh, and eighth commandments?

 12. What does God require in the ninth and tenth commandments?

 13. Can anyone keep the law of God perfectly?

 14. Did God create us unable to keep his law?

 15. Since no one can keep the law, what is its purpose?

 16. What is sin?

 17. What is idolatry?

18. Will God allow our disobedience and idolatry to go unpunished?

19. Is there any way to escape punishment and be brought back into God's favor?

20. Who is the Redeemer?

21. What sort of Redeemer is needed to bring us back to God?

22. Why must the Redeemer be truly human?

23. Why must the Redeemer be truly God?

24. Why was it necessary for Christ, the Redeemer, to die?

25. Does Christ's death mean all our sins can be forgiven?

26. What else does Christ's death redeem?

27. Are all people, just as they were lost through Adam, saved through Christ?

28. What happens after death to those not united to Christ by faith?

29. How can we be saved?

30. What is faith in Jesus Christ?

31. What do we believe by true faith?

32. What do justification and sanctification mean?

33. Should those who have faith in Christ seek their salvation through their own works, or anywhere else?

34. Since we are redeemed by grace alone, through Christ alone, must we still do good works and obey God's Word?

35. Since we are redeemed by grace alone, through faith alone, where does this faith come from?

36. What do we believe about the Holy Spirit?

 37. How does the Holy Spirit help us?

 38. What is prayer?

 39. With what attitude should we pray?

 40. What should we pray?

 41. What is the Lord's Prayer?

 42. How is the Word of God to be read and heard?

 43. What are the sacraments or ordinances?

 44. What is baptism?

 45. Is baptism with water the washing away of sin itself?

 46. What is the Lord's Supper?

 47. Does the Lord's Supper add anything to Christ's atoning work?

 48. What is the church?

 49. Where is Christ now?

 50. What does Christ's resurrection mean for us?

51. Of what advantage to us is Christ's ascension?

52. What hope does everlasting life hold for us?

For additional resources, see
www.newcitycatechism.com